REAL ESTATE INVESTMENT

A Beginner's Guide to Making Money in Real Estate

(A Comprehensive Guide on How to Locate and Profit From Real Estate)

Hobert Hammond

Published by Jackson Denver

Hobert Hammond

All Rights Reserved

ISBN 978-1-77485-237-8

Legal & Disclaimer

The information contained in this book is not designed to replace or take the place of any form of medicine or professional medical advice. The information in this book has been provided for educational and entertainment purposes only.

The information contained in this book has been compiled from sources deemed reliable, and it is accurate to the best of the Author's knowledge; however, the Author cannot guarantee its accuracy and validity and cannot be held liable for any errors or omissions. Changes are periodically made to this book. You must consult your doctor or get professional medical advice before using any of the suggested remedies, techniques, or information in this book.

Upon using the information contained in this book, you agree to hold harmless the Author from and against any damages, costs, and expenses, including any legal fees potentially resulting from the application of any of the information provided by this guide. This disclaimer applies to any damages or injury caused by the use and application, whether directly or indirectly, of any advice or information presented, whether for breach of contract, tort, negligence, personal injury, criminal intent, or under any other cause of action.

You agree to accept all risks of using the information presented inside this book. You need to consult a professional medical practitioner in order to ensure you are both able and healthy enough to participate in this program.

Table of Contents

Introduction

Congrats for making it this to this point! In this Concise Reads document will cover the most important aspects of closing. Although the aim of this article was to inform approximately 12 million prospective buyers and sellers of properties each year, it will never be a substitute for the specific advice given by your lender, agent attorney, accountant or attorney. Being informed means being prepared. Make a note of all questions you may have and ensure you have the answers prior to closing on the property. The learning never ceases and this is one of the most crucial decisions in your life. So be sure to keep asking questions.

In this article, we'll discuss about closing procedures. Do you realize that nearly 50% of buyers are shocked by the cost of closing? The process is easy but it might be a shock to discover closing costs make up 2-5percent of the selling cost of a property and, if you add the prepayment option, you're looking at 3 to 6 percent of the value of a house. These expenses are added on top of the initial downpayment. They may vary depending on whether the seller agrees to take a share of the closing costs.

The closing process could take several weeks or months following the signing of the purchase contract. In this article, we'll go over title transfer as well as title insurance inspections of homes as well as zoning laws. We'll also provide an inventory of all closing costs, possible tax deductions, and complete checklists for sellers and buyers that are based on all books in the series so to date.

In order to make us feel confident in the closing process to make sure we are comfortable, there are a few ideas we should be familiar with such as knowing what a survey of property is, and knowing how to get a deed on the property upon the closing. There are many different types of deeds that are in the same way, so it is important to be aware of the type of deeds we're paying for prior to diving into the various costs that come with settlement or closing. Bravo for pursuing this path of self-learning! Your knowledge is far over the common homeowner at this stage. We've only got a few other topics to be aware of, and by the time you've completed this final guide, you'll be able to know nearly everything that a Real Estate Agent who is newly licensed or perhaps more if you have an education in finance, accounting marketing, law, or design and construction of homes.

Chapter 1: What Does To Be A Successful Landlord?

In the beginning, what are the main reasons you're currently pursuing to be a landlord? Is the thought of owning your own an investment property and being a landlord your motivation? Or are you looking for an additional source of income? Do you have the practical managerial or business skills required to succeed in this field?

Oft, the notion of owning and renting a home is thought of as a simple method to boost the wealth of one's personal assets.However in order to succeed you must remember that it is a business endeavor and should be seen as it is. There's a lot more to it than purchasing a property and getting the rewards.It's essential to comprehend your motives to make better decisions , and less bad ones.

It can also assist you to determine which types of properties are most appealing to you since each comes with their own benefits and disadvantages.For instance as I've realized that owning residential rental properties is the best choice for me.It is simpler to find tenants in my neighborhood for residential units.Plus the rent covers the entire cost (mortgage and taxes, insurance and maintenance).And I like this type of job.

Commercial buildings are different types of rentals (warehouse as opposed to. retail).Personally I believe that these kinds of rentals are more difficult to keep.However I know numerous clients who believe exactly the opposite.Choose the one that is within your comfort zone.

Your personal style and goals can also play greatly when you decide the best option as well.Each kind of property ownership has advantages and potential risks to be productive. It is crucial to choose at an early stage whether you would like to concentrate on residential property or commercial office rentals and warehouses for commercial use excite you most? Or would a mix of both be the best option for you? Have a clear understanding of the requirements to own, lease and manage these properties.Then take action with this in your mind.

Residential is much different than the various types of commercial buildings.Without a passion for either area, you will not succeed.I have found it best to have a goal of where you want to be in five or ten years from starting.At this time, you can see if your plan can be attained in the timeframe you have set.Set REALISTIC expectations.Sometimes your plan might be more aggressive than what you want or the market in your area can sustain.Review your goals periodically and adjust as needed along your journey.

The most important thing to keep in mind when you are investing in real property is that the reputation of your company is crucial this is why it is crucial to make sure you find the right combination of tenants, contractors or realtors etc.Word will quickly spread if you're a landlord who isn't satisfied, fails to make the necessary changes or simply does not care.Go into the process knowing that you'll do your job to the highest of your abilities. You'll want to be able to perform well and earn the appreciation of your tenants. they don't just remain longer, but also suggest your properties to others.

Be aware of how important it is to keep track of the reputations of the people you collaborate with throughout this way.This is why it's important to choose a partner whom you trust.Through the years, you'll discover the perfect team that will be a benefit to you and one you are happy working with.Having a solid "team" can help you along the way.

Another option, when having a rental property to hire a property management firm like I use for my rentals.I work full-time in my "day work" and rely on the property management company to manage all of my daily tasks.The sole thing I manage is collecting rent as well as paying my mortgage.The option is yours to decide how many or how little from the occupations you wish to manage. The book will assist you in deciding what's most suitable for you.

Chapter 2: Non-Retirement Investment Accounts

Overview

Stocks, mutual funds CD'S, bonds, note, securities of business and many other assets are able to be liquidated to make cash to fund your business. If your private lenders aren't satisfied with the return they currently receive (which is quite likely in the current economic climate) If so, it might be worthwhile to talk with them about how to find out what it would require to transfer their cash into more flexible and easily accessible format.

The Positive

We all know that in the current economic climate, if people aren't happy with the return they getting from the above investment options, and they ought to be open and ready to speak with you. For those who have the majority of their assets with mutual funds they are usually familiar with not having to handle their assets any more than reading their monthly statement. This is also the case when the funds are invested in your account as the returns are guaranteed and do not require any effort from their side.

The Downside

The lender you choose to use will require them to liquidate their investment account and transfer funds into the money market or checking account prior to funds being able to be transferred to your deal. Keep in mind that numerous financial advisors, stock brokers and others. will attempt to hinder their clients from taking this risk (remember that nobody wants to lose their business?) by saying that their decision is dangerous. For some advisors, the primary reason is usually genuine concern for their clients and their lack of knowledge about the investment they have made and, of course, their inability to earn a profit from the investment.

Success Strategy

If you are a real estate investment it is essential to fully educate your potential investors on the advantages and disadvantages of your investment as compared to their current investments before soliciting them to transfer their money. The more knowledgeable your prospective client is, the less difficulty they'll have in moving their money, and the more faith they will have in the opportunity. Results and confidence will result in referrals and lenders.

Strategies #5: The Utilization of Equity in the Home Equity

Overview

It's true it is true that home equity is among the most neglected assets that anyone can have in their portfolio. Equity, just as your credit rating isn't "real" until it's converted into profits or gains of some kind. If you believe that you have 40 percent capital in the home, and it will make you feel financially secure however, the real estate market in your area decreases by 20 percent, what do you think about it now? Equity isn't very valuable unless utilized to your advantage.

If you're always making payments towards the principal balance of your mortgage to "build wealth" and have only a few available liquid assets that is not adding to your security. You're merely decreasing the risk for the mortgage company in the event of a market crash. You should note that your monthly installment doesn't decrease every month, as you pay principal reductions to your fixed-rate mortgage. Who really benefits here? I'm guessing it's certainly not the homeowner. If you are thinking that you might have to draw on the equity of your home in the event of financial emergencies be aware that the bank might not accept your request to safeguard their own interests (due to a decline in the market or indications that you've increased your risk of financial loss) as well as any additional payments you made on time to pay your principal are now not available to you, regardless of the circumstances.

This is a good idea: ask your lenders what rate you're giving them is more than the one they currently paying (or they would pay) for their mortgage. If you can answer "yes" then you should introduce them to the concept of "arbitrage" (see below for the Success Strategy below).

The Positive

It's a wonderful method to aid those who believed they were a complete waste of money. Many people view their home as a valuable asset, however it's not the case when it is a cost to them (taxes or insurance, for instance). If you can demonstrate to the people around you how you can earn a living off the equity in their home without putting their equity in danger it could change their lives for good.

The Downside

For the older generation that are older, it may be a challenging idea to break through their current beliefs about finances. Although they may earn some income out of air and their investment is secured by another property, some minds don't see that far outside the "box" which they were raised to live within. The majority of people live in a MUCH lesser quality of living than they're capable of, because they lack the financial skills to change certain things.

Another "downside" is that mortgages aren't so easy to obtain as they were in the past. The process can take quite a time, but the benefits are definitely greater than the disadvantages. Be aware that the recent financial meltdown and the financial crisis in this country have temporarily ended the availability of lines-of-credit on many local markets. A fixed-rate (non-LOC) loans aren't as effective in this kind of transaction because monthly interest payments are due from the borrower , even in the event that the money was not put into another investment. This could result in losses for the lender when they fail to put the money into an investment that could yield more of a return than the original loan.

Success Strategy

Arbitrage

Definition: A simultaneous acquisition and selling of an asset to gain from a change in the value. Also referred to as "risk lower profit".

Case Study

Michael as well as Susan both are nearing their mid-70's. They are are preparing for retirement. They have a few retirement savings and their house is clean and clear, however, they're worried that their savings as well as social security benefits aren't enough to cover the cost of living throughout their retirement. They're actually thinking about part-time jobs that can supplement the income (if you think this isn't the case, visit Wal-Mart and check out the staff at the front door) But Michael's health isn't the best and Susan is urging him to stay at home to take charge of him. They are unable to afford the rising health costs and are worried that any unexpected expenses could sabotage their retirement plans.

The Solution

Michael and Susan have heard about your investments in real estate notes from a mutual friend. They initially contacted you hoping that you would offer more of a return on their savings which is currently in a five-year CD. You ask them about their financial situation, and they voice their worries. They inform you of the equity in their home and you ask the mortgage company contact them. After a simple application, the lender decides that they can provide them with an option to borrow up to 70 percent of their home's market value. The appraiser estimates that the house is estimated to be worth

$300,000. A 70 percent line of credit could permit them to take advantage of up to $210,000 in capital at around 7percent.

Let's say that you have two deals that require a balloon note of $100,000 for a period of one year to purchase, renovate and refinance or let the house go to auction. You propose you to give Michael as well as Susan the sum of 2 points plus interest of 12%, due monthly, for financing the deals. Michael and Susan are willing to fund your deals . Susan immediately receive the 2 points fee once they have funded the deal, which amounts to $4000. Every month, they receive an interest payment of $2000 and pay on their credit line at $1,167, resulting in an overall income of 833. Through the course of the year, they make almost $10,000 in the amount of variation in interest payments, which is in addition to the fee of $4000 that they paid when closing. $14,000 is roughly what Michael was hoping to earn from a part-time job and now he can remain at home and relax and make the same money. When your deal is completed the loan is returned to principal, and their line of credit gets reduced to zero. Michael and Susan are willing to fund another deal for you and recommend to their former friends with similar financial circumstances.

Strategie #6: The Function Credit Cards Play in Private Lending

Overview

In spite of the criticisms about the dangers of credit cards, they are extremely efficient. It is a commonly ignored tool that could be utilized in real estate transactions. You or someone who you know have credit cards that have large credit lines that aren't used often. They're using them for "emergencies. Beyond that

You may also receive mailers of "0 percent for the month of March" on balance transfers , or even check accounts that can be used to purchase anything you need with a low transaction cost which are free of interest or a affordable interest (2.9 percent and so on.) for a set duration of time. You can use these offers on credit cards to your advantage and make use of to earn a profit?

The Positive

If you use them in the right manner when used correctly, credit cards can be an extremely affordable way to pay for deals. The fees for transactions can be at a minimum of $150 for an offer with 0% interest and, if they are paid back within the time frame specified they can allow you to pay for your purchases almost completely free.

The Downside

Everyone now is aware that credit cards include numerous tiny "trap doors" clauses that could make your fantastic deal an unwise deal if observed carefully. This 0% discount could increase retroactively to a 30- percent interest rate when you fail to pay the minimum amount by just one day. In addition, if you are unable to make the payment by the time the introductory rate ends or, at a minimum, transfer the balance to a different credit card, you could end up paying more than the real estate purchase could afford.

Success Strategy

You can also consider using other credit cards for financing that is only short-term. If a card is offering an initial rate for 12 months, make sure you only use the card to secure an offer that you could easily sell or re-finance in less than 6 months.

Make the minimum payment on your credit card that will be debited automatically into your account on a regular basis at least one week prior to the date when the payment is due. This reduces the risk of not making a payment and causing the interest rate to increase.

After you've financed your purchase by using a credit or debit card, make sure you don't use it to make any purchases at all until the credit card is fully paid. The purchases made will be charged at the normal rate for purchases that is usually between 8% and 21%. The minimum payments you pay for will be transferred to the most expensive balance that you have on the card and not to the credit balance that is introductory. Credit cards are a fantastic option to leverage arbitrage in your favour. If you have a high-limit card you own or not, make use of others' cards to finance your purchases and allow them to earn additional income.

Case Study:

Rachel has discovered a wonderful bargain on a bank-owned property. The property has an ARV (after repair value) of $200,000 and she's signed a contract to purchase the home for $100,000. She'll need to finish the work of $20,000 to bring the home up to the standard of retail however, she has already found buyers on Craigslist who is qualified for an FHA loan worth $185,000 and offered $165,000 to purchase the house after the renovation is completed.

Rachel has an individual lender named Christopher who will lend her $100,000 to purchase the home but she doesn't have additional funds to pay for the rehabilitation of the home. Christopher will pay for the loan with his IRA and will not need monthly payments. Rachel proposes the possibility of paying Christopher 1.5 points, and also 12% of accrued interest on a balloon of 12 months and Chris agrees.

Rachel contacts her buddy Trevor who has credit cards with high limits that he's not using. Rachel proposes to Trevor the opportunity to earn 3 points plus 15% in interest on the payment of a balloon note for 6 months worth $30,000. She requests an additional $10,000 to pay for her 1.5 points ($1,500) which she was willing to give Susan to cover the $100,000 note, as well as the 3 points she'll be paying Trevor ($900) as well as an account for reserve of $2250 which will provide six months of monthly interest payment for Trevor at a rate of $375 per month. Trevor asked that Rachel make monthly payments to ensure that he doesn't need to pay out of pocket to pay the payments on his credit card to repay the loan.

Rachel has now paid for the entire purchase as well as the rehab and has paid the financing costs to the lenders in at the beginning, and has an additional $5,350 in her account to cover any unanticipated expenses due to the project.

Rachel's renovation contractor completed the project six weeks after the purchase, however, her buyer can't close on the purchase for 90 days from the date on which she bought it because of "seasoning conditions" for the purchaser's FHA loan. The buyer is required to move into the house immediately and lease the property from Rachel until he's able to finish closing his loan. He is required to pay $1200 per month for rent until the closing day 91. Rachel's total interest cost will be $4,125 over the course of the 90 day loan less the rent of $1,800 she earned during the period. This is equivalent to the net cost of holding $2,325. Rachel will sell her home for $165,000, less the $5,000 closing cost and her total payment to each lender of $134,125 and rents of $1,800. This amounts to an overall net profit for Rachel in the amount of $27.675. The return on investment for Rachel is unlimited, as she has not invested any of her own funds.

Her first lending institution, Christopher, received a tax-free return on Christopher's Roth IRA in the amount of $4,500 in just 90 days. This was an annualized yield of 18.

The second lender of Rachel, Trevor, paid a $150 transaction fee to his credit card company in order to get the $30,000 was granted to Rachel and paid no charges since he was on an introductory rate of 0.

Trevor got three points ($900) and interest for three months at 15 percent ($1,125) for an total amount of $2,025 less $150 transaction fee was paid for, resulting in an income of $1,875 within 90 days. Trevor's annualized return was unending since he did not use any of his own funds.

Rachel's buyer managed to buy a beautifully renovated house for just $35,000 less than its the market value. Rachel was delighted to accept since she's not a shrewd buyer, and is aware that the phrase "fast nickel is better than the slow dime".

Everyone wins! !

Chapter 3: Investment Properties

Investment properties are properties that you believe you could renovate or an investment in the property, and then rent it out. There are times when they're worth looking at in areas where rental rates are especially lucrative. It is essential to know the speed at which agents plan to rent their properties out within the vicinity of the property, because when the property is vacant, it's making you money. If, however, you thought of investing in a long-term property investment, it will require little effort and you will be capable of turning the property around quickly. The best way to can make it a profitable investment is by purchasing the property at a fair price , and knowing what monthly mortgage payments will be for each month. It is then necessary to compare the cost with the amount of rental you can reasonably anticipate from the property each month. The ideal scenario is when the rent is enough to cover mortgage due to the fact that the property you own is ownership of the property which eventually pays for the property.

It is a great way to make an investment if you have large funds and would like to make an ongoing income from a property. It will pay you a regular amount each month, but it is important to determine the terms of your the lease and ensure that everything is covered by an agreement legally binding which requires the tenant to pay an initial premium at the start of their tenancy. This is to compensate for any damages that may have occurred to the property in the course of their use within the premises.

If you are considering the possibility of investing in properties like this, it is important to be aware of the following aspects:

What is the current demand for rental properties in this region?

What is the maximum amount of rent that could be derived through the investment?

What kind of repairs are required and how much will they cost?

How fast do you plan to give the property over to tenants?

Keep in mind that for the entire time you are the owner of the property, you have the responsibility to insure the property , and it costs cash. Tenants are accountable for the insurance of their personal property inside the home however, you'll have to determine the cost to get public liability insurance as well as a complete household insurance that covers every eventuality. If you're planning to invest in a number of homes, a blanket insurance policy from an insurance company could reduce your expenses and you can shop around and search for discounts, but be sure that the coverage is sufficient and that you do not be liable in the case that there is a fire or damage on the home.

The mortgage cannot be transferred to another person. The property is yours. Even if the property isn't being let out to tenants and you are required to pay the monthly installments. Therefore, it is important to have a contingency fund in place to cover the rent should a tenant fails to pay the rent or at times when the property is not occupied by an occupant.

When you're deciding on homes for this kind in market could see that there are some fantastic homes for rentals during the holidays because the location is ideal for vacations . If that is the case you might find a bargain on a vacation rental home or apartment that someone would not like anymore or was foreclosed due to not paying the mortgage due. Foreclosures offer a chance because they are typically sold by banks for the amount owed instead of selling them at their commercial value.

You'll need to consider the needs to be made to the home and the amount it will cost. Make sure that you're informed of this prior to when you buy the property. Therefore, you might need to borrow higher than the price of the property to cover the necessary repairs to bring the house back on rent. Many people who have owned an apartment for a period of time are looking to dispose of it since changes in their lives and now they don't wish to own a home in the region. It could also be because they the property is not able to make the work required to bring the home up to standards.

When you go to a place like this it's important to determine what rental being offered by other properties within the same location and also determining the cost needed to upgrade the property to the standard demanded by the current generation of tourists and visitors. Compare similar properties. It is important to present your property in a way that entices people to visit and if you aren't sure that you're able to do this, it might be wise to leave and continue exploring instead of purchasing an unprofitable home that does not generate enough revenue to cover the mortgage. The benefit of the option of letting out for vacation is that rents will always be more expensive than residential properties however you need to be aware that when you rent out your home for short periods there is a need to tidy the property between leases and you'll have to keep track for all your lets. You can hire an agency to manage this, but you have to consider the fact that they charge for their services. Be sure to weigh all of this prior to making a decision to sign up for a vacation rental as you must be able to view the whole picture. You may discover that while summer months are rewarding however, winters aren't always as good.

Chapter 4: Make a Invest in You

One thing that truly changed my life is that if you want succeed in the world of today whatever you do, or in any venture you're in it is essential to put your money into yourself first. Are you sure? If you don't know how to proceed What do you think? You'll never achieve where you want to be. Therefore, investing in who you wants to become and the direction you'd like to go is crucial since it allows you to enjoy the life you've always envisioned.

And now, I'll beg you to answer. What do you want to find? What is the reason you are reading this book? One thing I find very important in real estate, just as in any other business, is that for you to succeed you must possess the proper mentality. Should you choose real estate as the thing you'd like to be doing then you must say to yourself that you are an ESTATE INSURER.

Every day, you should awake and declare that you are A REAL ESTATE INSURER. What's likely to take place is that you're going to begin seeing things you've never seen before. You'll begin to believe the things you're declaring. Everyone who succeeds says these words to themselves. I've heard that when professional baseball players come to bat they envision that they are Babe Ruth or whoever their favorite childhood hero was. It is exactly the same thing if are looking to succeed in whatever field you choose.

You'll drive or walk down the road and start seeing homes with grass right as high as your knees and windows that are broken, and you've have never noticed them prior to now. In a flash you're trying to determine what's going on behind the house or property. You'll begin asking neighbors about the history of the house next door . I'm sure they'd love to have that house fixed up and sold faster than you would. The old, shabby house has lowered their property value and causing problems for the community and could even be causing harm to their children. If you purchase a brand new car, and you're driving back home from the dealership you see that exact car more often than you have ever before. This is known as the Baader Meinhof phenomenon. It's a trick your brain performs on your mind when you show the time to look into something. When you notice something that you're interested in it will trigger your brain to bring up the things that match your interests. They're almost like small answers. But, you need to make your mind believe that you are looking for it first , and then be convinced. This is what happens when you alter your thinking as you become more clear about what you're seeking and once you've achieved this, you'll be more successful.

The business may drive your mind yet nevertheless, it's extremely rewarding. This is why I'm asking you to think about it again. What are you searching for?

Chapter 5: Now that I've Priced it, how do I Market It?

Have you noticed that some houses in the same area seem to be left on the market while other homes are placed into escrow In a matter of minutes? Why does this occur?

There are homes that are priced incorrectly and anyone could sell a home that is priced way too low. However, selling a house for the highest price regardless of the market easy as well. It is important to find that one person who is interested in the home enough to purchase it for the price you're willing to offer itfor, or even higher!

So if it's this easy Why isn't everyone doing it? It all boils down to selling and marketing ability.When the beautiful completely furnished FSBO house down the street is being advertised for sale in nine months, and the typical home just a few doors away and priced higher is owned by a new owner, you can witness the difference in how homes sell themselves.

You could give away all the hot doggies, cookies, bottled doughnuts and water you like at open houses, but there's only a certain number of people who will take an interest in the home.You might try to follow the same thing as agents and try to get as many potential buyers as you can through the door.They believe that if enough people look at it, then someone is likely to purchase the property.

This method can be time-consuming and frequently leads to frustration, and sometimes price reductions. If you've had 100 showings but no offers, agents are likely to reduce the price. A majority of sellers will to be frustrated.

I would begin by looking at potential buyers who visited the property to be sure they are the right buyer for you, and 2They saw what they anticipated to see while touring the property (no surprises due to inaccurate photos) 3. They were aware of the price and the terms prior to viewing.

Your agent or you must identify the distinctive particularity of your property and then create a master marketing strategy that has the objective of identifying the buyer who is willing , and willing to pay for the feature you're providing.

I found a property for sale on four bedroom 1.5 bath home that was constructed in 1954.The house was quite small , and by small I mean less than 1400 square feet.It was home to what is now shoebox-sized rooms, tiny storage spaces, as well as a chaotic layout.

My clients had lived in the property for over 20 years.They purchased it with little improvement and only a few improvements when we decided to sell this house.Original windows, bathrooms with outdated tiles and flooring, original kitchen cabinets, etc.

The homes that were comparable that were recently sold and for sale have been upgraded with granite counter-tops and stainless appliances, as well as dual paned windows, and fresh paint.

The price I set for my home was exactly the same way as other houses, however I advertised it based on the size of the lot alone.I didn't pay attention to the dimensions of rooms or windows.We did not mention any of those and emphasized the massive property size.Our lot was approximately 1,000 square feet bigger than many of the homes in the area.We discovered one buyer who was more concerned about the size of the lot and the lack of any upgrades. The home sold for all asking price and was among the most popular selling homes in the area.

I was unable to place this property on an ad on Sunday along alongside similar properties then price it the way I did and see the similar results.My advertised property didn't stand up.I needed to figure out the elements that made this property distinctive and then promote the property in accordance with its distinctiveness.

I advertised the benefits of the property and explained the various possibilities with a property of that is of that size. At the end of the day I found buyers willing to pay for what my clients wanted and then the transaction was closed.

There was another time when I sold a distinct property located in 29 Palms California.The property was a 3 bedroom house which was laid out so that bedrooms and bathrooms were distinct unit.In fact, you needed to go back into the main house via the entrance of the master and then take few steps onto the patio.

The peculiarity of the house, I discovered that the basement is actually an underground bomb shelter that was constructed during the wartime.

The unusual floorplan was not mentioned in any advertisements However, I did mention the bomb shelter.Again I discovered one buyer enthusiastic over the uniqueness in the shelter and the home was sold.

A while ago, I dealt with one of my clients who purchased an apartment in a brand new development located in an inland area. There were several condominiums with similar floorplans within the development, however she decided to put in an offer on one that was priced at $30,000 more than the other properties.

Why was a house with the same floor plan, similar appliances, with the same interior decor , etc. was priced at $30,000 more expensive and what made her be so eager to buy it? It was a spectacular views from the master bedroom , and she could see all up to the sea. She could imagine herself relaxing every morning drinking a cup coffee in the morning before working while watching the sunrise.

The Sellers placed a premium on the view because it was exclusive to the specific unit.My customer was prepared to shell out $35,000 premium for the unique view. And she did.

Sometimes , as in the case of the old house the home isn't even focused on the house.I have advertised the lot.You pay attention to the feature(s) or benefit(s) that make your property apart from the rest.Once you know the characteristic and you choose the most likely buyers , and you create your marketing to target them.

If you follow this strategy, this strategy will not only help you be able sell your house faster however, you'll also be able to sell it at a premium price and without price cuts.

It is important not to have a thousand feet wandering around the home.Your objective should be to attract one buyer who is qualified willing, able and ready to buy the home.Develop plans for each property to connect with that buyer and achieve your target.

Setting the Stage for a Sales

If you're satisfied with the price you paid then it's time to get back to the independent opinion you sought earlier.What areas require improvement or repairs?

The following three aspects you need to consider for optimal pricing:

1-Decluttering

2-Repairs

3-Staging

I've represented a lot of buyers who requested appointments to view houses based on photos that were uploaded to the MLS.When we drove up to the house, the customers did not want to leave the vehicle. What was the reason?

Old paint cans and lawnmowers littered the yard; the green grass that was featured in the photos had turned brown over time and toys for kids were scattered across the path and oil pans that had escaped were leaking from autos while fences fell.

You only have one chance to make an impression So, make sure your front clean and sharp.Trim the shrubs and trees and then mow the lawn. continue to water and make sure that your children tidy up their toys.

If you see a lot of potted plants, or even small items on the outside or in the back cut down on the number so the area doesn't look like a mess to an outsider. Be sure that the front entrance is clear of spider webs and dirt.

If you have vinyl siding, it is possible to clean it with pressure or have someone else take care of it.Fix the fences to ensure that the garden is safe and finally If the paint is peeling, chipping or flaking it will need to be addressed too.

Cleaning up the exterior is typically an easy task and doesn't cost a lot of cash unless you're looking for an exterior paint job. Therefore, invest time cleaning things up to get potential customers in the to the.

After a prospective buyer has entered the house, you'll want buyers to feel a sense of an open space.In some instances, this could be achieved through changing or moving furniture.In other situations, this might require removing furniture entirely.

Many of us have photos and other ornaments around the house to create a sense of homey-ness, but the majority of us don't sell our home.The house you're selling is different from the house where you are living.Buyers don't want to view your personal belongings, which is why you'll want to get rid of everything which hold their memories.

The thought of removing clutter causes you to feel anxious, imagine it as packing. Get rid of any extra photos and displays of collections magazines, books, etc. The home a prospective buyer would like to visit is not always the same home in which you're living in.

The purpose of a ready home is to change the interior so that buyers are unable to tell the type of person who lives there.By taking a look at the décor, you shouldn't be able to immediately tell whether the residents are elderly or a single male or even an professional couple.

What is the situation with interior carpeting and paint? The chances are that the prospective buyers of your home are likely to paint and maybe installing flooring.So it can be dealt with in two ways.If you're a fan of particular hues throughout your homeYou know, vibrant reds, yellows greens, and so on... Paint your walls with neutral shades. Take down wallpapers or old wallpaper, including panelling and faux brick.

Neutral colors allow buyers to see walls as a blank canvas' and aid in visual perception space.Bright colors might be attractive to some people, but off-putting or off-putting to another.Also certain brighter hues or even wall coverings can make the room appear smaller.

In certain areas, carpeting is not the norm.For some time, laminate flooring was trendy, and followed by wood floors, and finally tile and tile that appears as if wood has taken over.

If your flooring is not able to stand an effective cleaning, that is, it's that it is permanently stained or has the smell of smoke or pet odor it is best to change it out with something simple and functional.If you decide to invest in high-end carpeting, or install laminate flooring, buyers might decide to tear it up and replace it with something that fits their preferences.

But, most importantly don't place more money into your home than you are likely to take out.In the real world, price doesn't always translate to value.If you decide to install hardwood flooring, you aren't able to include this to your price.If you've installed a new, decent neutral-colored carpet, the value that carpeting brings to your home could be worth the amount it will cost to purchase the carpet and get it installed.Bottom rule of thumb is to not be too extravagant.

It's important to be aware of how to ensure that your home is as good as it can be with no being too much improving.Do small fixesAdd GFI's to bathrooms and kitchens, check sure that outlets are working and that outlet covers are in place repair leaky faucets and toilets, ensure that all appliances are working, and switch light bulbs to new lighting .... You'll get the idea.

If you're unsure of what features your house might require or require, you could always seek an inspection by a professional. The inspector will go out and examine everything like you would if you bought the home.You could then go on and make repairs to one or more things to improve quality of life in your home.As an added benefit for buyers who are interested the potential buyer, you can request an report of the inspection to show the condition of the property.

Don't go out and buy new state of the latest appliances such as home theatre systems tankless water heaters other such items since you likely won't get your money back from the sale price. In the present you're making sure you are taking care of the basics and cleaning the place up.

Or not to Stage or Not to

Furniture-equipped homes tend to sell faster than homes houses without furniture. The longer a property is for sale, the more the seller has to pay for carrying expenses, including utility bills, mortgage payments and maintenance etc.So when looking to stage a home that is vacant homeowners should consider the expense of staging as opposed to. the cost associated with a prolonged period of time being on the market.

Staging is the process of the process of adding or removing furniture and items to make the house more appealing to prospective buyers.Homeowners might choose to hire professional stagers to help with this, or for lower-end properties, they could include a few simple staging techniques to enhance the look and ambience of the house.

Everything is decluttered and staging is no exception.Less is more and the excess items are removed from the home to let potential buyers imagine the home's space.In the case of a house that is empty there is a minimum amount of carefully placed furniture and other items are placed inside the home to provide an impression of the space and flow of the design.

The colors are soothing and neutral furniture is designed to make rooms appear more spacious and inviting.Lighting is essential to create an atmosphere of warmth and ease.

If your home is equipped, a Stager might be able to make use of what's already in hand.You are likely to be surprised by the changes which can be created by simply rearranging and eliminating items that are there.You are able to find simple staging methods that you can apply yourself by searching for staging ideas on the internet or browsing through magazines.

If you decide to delegate everything to professionals The cost of staging will be based on the magnitude and scope of job.A consultation could cost only one hundred dollars however staging a large house could cost thousands of dollars.Staging the vacant house may be as little as 1 percent of the asking price, however, when you look at the statistics that show the homes that are staged sell at average 3% higher than homes that have not been staging, it might be a good idea to consider investing in.

The last thing to consider to present a property will be yourself.Whether your selling the home FSBO or working with an agent, prepare to be courteous and friendly taking only those questions being asked of you.

Do not share with the agent and/or buyer the story of your life or the story of the house.If you're a talkative person and also an "open to the world," you will need to pull it in.It is nice to be friendly, however knowing is the key to success in the sales process, and the more you inform a potential buyer or agent about yourself and your reasons for moving in, the more likely you are to weaken your negotiation position.

If you are forced to sell, don't reveal to anyone that you hate to sell, but are facing foreclosure. This kind of information will surely result in lower offers. The buyers will begin to research the amount of debt owed on the property, rather than its fair market value since they know that you need to get it sold fast.They will seek to take advantage of conditions.

If you've already bought another house, if you need to relocate due to work, or if you've relocated into an assisted-living facility don't inform the buyer. Buyers is likely to notice "need to dispose of" indications and your offers are most likely to be low.The more detail you give regarding the reasons for your sale greater the reason they'll have to present a lower price.

If you're at the home to greet prospective buyers when they visit the property, please put yourself in another room, or go for an outing.

You should be prepared to answer questions about the many wonderful improvements you've completed as well as the condition of your home.But only answer when you are asked keep it on the subject.

I represent clients who are divorcing frequently I do not inform the other agent or buyer about the circumstances.Again divorce is usually a sign of that you must sell your home now, therefore, it's not talked about.

There are a few points you could mention which could be helpful. If someone asks you if is there any offer available, you could respond with "we are looking at each offer this Saturday (or choose an date)."You're making it clear if there are or don't exist any offers, but you're informing them of the deadline.

If you have any other questions regarding pricing flexibility or your main objective, you can reply with "we have been carefully evaluating every deal when we receive it.We haven't considered the need to sell at a lower cost."

Be courteous, but remain vague.If you're represented, it is possible to direct all inquiries to your agent, so that you don't be uncomfortable.

Sweetening the Pot

If you are in a market that is slow. You've already set the price for your property, and buyers are trickling in and you have to decide if you're offering incentives in exchange for a full price or an offer that is higher and quick close or both.What is the meaning of incentives? Just a small amount to create the feeling that the buyer is they have to make immediately with an offer.

An incentive could be

- a decorating allowance

- up to a month of the HOA's dues (if your property is HOA that is associated to it),

The remainder of the calendar year for alarm services

The remainder of the property taxes,

--etc.

You can get the picture. Some thing that will ensure that the buyer is enticed to put into the offer in full ASAP.Something that makes buyers feel they're receiving something worth their money as well as a wonderful house.

The incentives listed are lower than the typical closing cost contribution as well as the incentive program could create an auction where you may receive multiple bids and can sell for more than the price of the property.

If you receive multiple attractive offers, it is important to make an offer to every buyer, informing them that you've received several offers and ask each one to submit their most expensive and Best offer within the deadline that is very precise.

It is recommended to request the highest and most desirable price since the most attractive offer you get might be more than the price at which you could have responded. In the event of a multiple offer, it's best for the agent who is listing to engage with the selling agent to establish the level of interest of every buyer.

If a potential buyer is interested in the house but thinks there are some people they can live with, then that would likely not be the person who you wish to finalize the deal.You prefer a buyer who has fallen in love certain aspects of the home and can visualize the Christmas tree that will be in the family room or the weekend barbecues together with relatives as well as friends.The more a potential buyer loves the home and the property, the more they will be willing to pay, but the less likely they will not to withdraw from the escrow.

Chapter 6: What Changed in Real Estate In 2008?

"Real estate doesn't go down" was often proclaimed in the financial press in 2005 and in 2006. This wasn't the case for a long time. The majority of people didn't realize that the current state of the market for real estate was not sustainable.

A good friend of mine worked as a salesperson for pest control for new high-end houses in the year the year 2006. I was told about visiting a stunning four-bedroom house that was conversing with the owner in detail about the condition of the market for real estate. The owner of the house proudly claimed that speculation in the real estate market was the cause of his excellent living space, and that he was in need of pest control services, however it was not enough money during the month as he was desperate to raise funds to purchase a luxury waterfront house. I was often thinking about the gentleman I've did not meet, and reminisced at the thought of the hardships the man must have endured during the years and months that followed.

Many people were lured by the promises of quick money and huge wealth by investing in real property. The financial "experts" on the cable news channels praised the value and security of real property. The first time I saw them was Jim Rogers on the Saturday morning Fox News shows, standing on his own as the sole voice of reason telling viewers that "this will get ugly". Unfortunately, the majority of viewers did not have Jim's insight and ended up being taken to the bathroom. The most intelligent people were waiting for the right time in anticipation of the day when real estate would become an asset that was prone to destruction and they could get almost everything they wanted for inexpensive.

I witnessed some amazing purchases in 2008. A few of my dearest acquaintances have been Realtors and they were operating in one of the most battered down areas in America in the metro Detroit market. The deals I heard about shocked me and I had been waiting for this opportunity for several years.

I relocated to Florida in the midst of the financial crisis and quickly got acquainted with others who were in the field. A mortgage professional I know purchased a 32-unit apartment building for half what it sold for a year before. Another friend of mine purchased a 54 unit Class B townhouse situated in Brandon, Florida, a decent middle class neighborhood, using owner financing for only $4500 in down.

Although both deals caused some envy in the moment I believe I achieved the best of them all. When I lived in Michigan I owned three rental homes in working-class suburbs. I resisted acquisition in the year 2004 when I was waiting to take on something bigger. I was sure that the market crash could provide me with that chance and it did.

I bought an 88-unit property with owner financing and was able get commercial financing in 2010 thanks to the huge equity I had built up within the property. I employed the method I'll be sharing with the readers in chapter 5 and am excited to try this method time and time again. Being able to communicate with potential buyers is crucial. Understanding how to behave when you're on the receiving end is crucial to closing deals that make you a better prospect for the future.

I can see the next downturn becoming even more profitable and full of opportunities as well as a longer time period to profit from these opportunities. It will be the most lucrative three years in our lives to invest in real estate and astounding fortunes could be made.

If you're only able to remember one thing from this book, keep in mind that you can purchase multifamily properties during this downturn without any down payment and with just the smallest amount of money, you can purchase virtually everything.

I would rather own multifamily properties rather than single family residences for reasons I'll go over in the next chapter. In 2008, after I moved to Florida homes located in St. Petersburg that were listed for sale for $150,000 were listed at $30,000. This is the equivalent of a 500%

decrease in value! Do you want to have five rental homes with paying tenants and one with the same rental rate (and 1/5 of the total income) like the other houses for the same $150,000? Is that even worthwhile to ask? There will always be a need for a place to rent a couple of bedroom homes within St. Petersburg. In retrospect I would have used that chance. I wouldn't be trying to sell them today, just like I'm looking to market my building.

When I was preparing to selling my property in Michigan I was looking at markets in Tampa. I knew that I would soon be moving to Tampa and knew that this overconfident Florida market could provide excellent chances to purchase a good property for a low price. My research did not serve any reason, however, because the prices were ridiculous and I found myself thinking I was wrong in times of weak points. Prices were skyrocketing and there did not appear to be any slowing down. I was constantly reminding myself that the wages were not rising and that at these rates real estate wasn't an investment worth making.

I called at a few properties to get a feel for the market in a way and was lucky and met an old friend who was more than willing to share some advice. "You are aware that we had an economic crash in the real estate market in the year 1990 and this one could be a lot more severe." The veteran vet added. In the past, advertisements for apartment buildings had caps of 4percent. The old timer laughed and stated "I would never even consider buying a new one until I buy it for 10 times my earnings (a cap rate of 10%)." Then I thought "wouldn't this be fantastic". I didn't realize that the old man was able to offer 10% cap rates to pick from in abundance.

What type of PROPERTY to buy?

BUYING HOUSES

Single-family homes give you the most convenient opportunity to purchase property with absolutely no cost. There is a lot of opportunity commercial real estate properties to purchase without putting cash down and with a little time, and you'll be capable of picking and choosing when you're in this Golden Age when it comes to homes. For us, the best bargains to be found will be found in the type of homes that are ideal for renting out. Smaller starter homes and single-family homes won't have any buyers and are likely to experience the highest number of foreclosures.

When the time comes to buy and, with a bit of due diligence, you'll in a position to determine who's in trouble in relation to their mortgage (or their taxes in the event that they don't own an mortgage) and you'll be able to assist the person out of a difficult circumstance. If someone is a homeowner and doesn't pay their taxes on their property and the lender steps into the picture and help them keep the property from being sold for the County. Although there is a wealth of gold to mine with REO property that bank need to purchase and purchase a property from someone who is driven and does not have a mortgage can be an excellent chance.

It is possible to get that dream house at a bargain price, however there is a lot of competitors, so I'd suggest focusing your efforts on creating wealth from this once-in-a-lifetime opportunity. You'll be able to make a fortune in cash flow when you provide rental housing for renters for many decades to come. There are also opportunities to earn significant capital gains if decide to sell the property 10 years from now However, I'm cash-strapped and will make the most of this opportunity to stay full of cash for the duration of my future years.

Do your homework now. Find out where the most suitable schools district for this kind housing for your town. Make a list of the neighborhoods you'd like to put housing for, and then become acquainted with the properties in the area. Keep track of what the current prices for sales are to ensure you are aware of the kind of deal you'll get. Plan to pay at minimum 50percent less than the price you're currently paying for your property.

The main benefit of a single-family home as an investment in real estate is that it's the most liquid kind of property when it's time to sell. Another benefit is that there will be no tenant disputes, which often happen from time to the time when you own a multifamily home. It's also important to remember that everyone will need housing and a modest but dependable housing is always a good demand.

Purchase DUPLEXES and TRIPLEXES, as well as FOURPLEXES.

Multifamily homes with four units or less have one major advantagethe ability to buy using a mortgage for residential use. This won't be of much value to you right now, or in the future but that's not too bad in the grand scheme of things.

This is a tip that you can utilize to your advantage during the coming recession of deflation. The owners of fourplexes and duplexes generally don't have huge pockets. There are some certain exceptions, but the majority owners of these homes will be in a bind and will have bills to pay. You'll see a lot of homeowners who bought these homes at the peak of their value and are desperate to find an exit.

It's an ideal area to capitalize. It's also the place the time to be ready. With just a few dollars it is possible to obtain owner financing and set what price pay. Imagine yourself in the shoes of the seller. He is the owner of a property that in which he's failed. It's likely impacted the way he lives in a negative way. The economy is down and fear has risen. "How do I pay my mortgage? What amount of interest will I be required to pay in the event that I fail to make my credit card bill?" Consider how much 1,000 dollars and a way out will be to someone like this during their time in a time of crisis. Think about how excited you'll feel to "give" the property to you in exchange for that.

If the Golden Age kicks off, I wouldn't recommend ever paying more than $1000 to obtain the ownership of a single-family house or multifamily home with four unit or less. If the owner in distress is asking for or demands more than that, just go on to the next one.

BUILDING APARTMENTS FOR SALE

It took me several years in the field of real estate to get this figured out however, apartments are an ideal choice for those who want for a stake in the real property. Everyone will require an area to live in but they may not necessarily require an office space or even a space to rent for their business, or self storage facility. No matter what technology replaces the old, the people will always require an area to live in. In the current recession affordable homes will be in high demand. Luxury, stylish and expensive homes will not.

Maintaining a budget is crucial, since the net operating profit which is also known as NOI, that your property can generate will determine how much the value of your property will be. As you grow your investment portfolio, it's important to see that having a portfolio comprised of single-family houses will result in management costs that can reduce the margins. If your entire income is in theory in one place and you can save significant amounts in the expense of managing.

Let's say that one investor constructs a portfolio that includes 10 single-family homes, while another investor acquires the building of a 10-unit apartment. The investor who owns 10 single family homes has 10 roofs and 10 yards to keep, whereas the apartment owner has the one. Additionally, there is the administration expense of owning 10 properties and the potential exposure to vacant properties.

The cost of vacancy is the largest expense for landlord. In order to put it into perspective, if you own one family of tenants who rent at $1,000 per month, and the house is empty for a month each year, it's losing $1000 for the year due to vacant. In a time span of 10 years it could result in losing $10,000. Sorry if this seems normal sense or unnecessary, but if you have a single-family property and it becomes vacant there is no revenue If you own several units in one place, vacant spaces don't hurt you bottom line.

Another reason why apartments are great for investment vehicles. For residential properties, which includes multifamily properties with 4 unit or less worth of your property will be determined on comparable sales, also known as comps.

Commercial real estate is where its value will be determined only on the revenue it earns. If you own a multi-family commercial property There are many options to increase your revenue and cut costs. Opportunities to accumulate enormous equity are plentiful.

A quality multi-family property can bring an impressive return while assuming an extremely low amount of risk. After you've built equity in the investment, financing from commercial sources can be very easy to obtain. In the event of purchasing a property without a financial institution and establishing an equity position prior to obtaining financing is the most efficient path to wealth that I've found after years of looking and researching. Income from passive sources is most important factor to building wealth and apartment homes "are special assets that could provide significant passive income throughout the course the time.

If you think single-family homes appealing, or you're more comfortable having a lovely triplex or duplex, then do not hesitate to take your time and follow your passion. After you have read chapters 5-6, however you are able to skip these types of homes and jump right into the thrilling world that is owning commercial property. In addition, you will be able to own the property and take control of it without the risk of needing to work with an institution, and also have the chance to build enormous capital for your own. What's more satisfying than this?

Chapter 7: To Pay for It

Once you've scouted and discovered a shabby duckling property you believe is something you are able to work with The next step is to find the method of paying for it in a way that makes sense to you. If you don't want to cash out in advance to purchase the property you're buying, there are a variety of choices to pick from when you are looking to get another person to purchase the investment property. Before you begin exploring each one however, it's essential to do some research first to make sure you understand what you're getting yourself into.

Being a good borrower

Particularly, this means you'll need to be aware of the tools you're working with when you are trying to get funding. This means that you're likely be required to begin by examining your credit score and then seek out professional assistance when you believe you're not in the position at where you'd like to be. It's not the only thing you'll have know about but the effects of the Great Recession means that it is much harder to secure a loan to invest in property than it was in the past. This is particularly the case if you don't possess much experience with investing or have a long history of credit. The word "difficult" doesn't necessarily mean impossible however, particularly in the event that you approach potential lenders by stating:

A substantial down payment: These days banks are expected to insist that you put at least 20 percent of total value of the property as a down payment and hard money lenders may require more than that, you'll discover that if you even pay five percent above the minimum amount, you'll begin to see lower rates in a matter of minutes. A higher percentage overall of the value of the property can be an excellent way to convince institutions to ignore small negative marks on your credit however this can only go so far.

If you're unable to pay at least 20 percent of the cost of the home, even though you are eligible to get a loan from a financial institution the best option is to secure a pair of mortgages for the property instead of only one. This can be more challenging than getting one mortgage however it's likely will reduce the overall profit of your business. If you decide to taking this route, it is suggested to try to settle one of the mortgages as fast as you can.

Be aware of where you stand: Once you've done your homework and looked up your score on credit, you'll be able to get an idea of what you can anticipate regarding the interest rates for any loans that you manage to obtain. Anything less than 740 will cost you more per month in the event that you want to maintain the same rate of interest that someone who has the highest possible credit score. In particular, this will be the case that you'll usually pay two points more for each 10 points below 740 what your credit score is. If you do not want to pay a high amount of monthly payments , then you'll be required to pay a higher interest rate. These are the two alternatives.

Furthermore, you're likely be required to attend any meeting with a prospective lender with an up-to current assessment of all your investment and personal expenses in the last six months and proof that you are able to afford each one costs for at least six months in the time. If you own multiple rental properties, you'll need to demonstrate that you are able to cover all the related costs for the full six-month period as well.

Find out who to talk to If your finances aren't in the best condition they might be, or you're able to put down a lower overall amount to invest in the property, it's important to stay away from the bigger financial institutions and look at the local alternative instead. Smaller credit unions in the local area typically have rules that are more flexible in terms of the requirements for lending, particularly in the event that you'll invest in the local region. They have a greater interest in seeing the whole local area grow which means you'll be able to get more without spending more.

In addition, you will discover that the request for owner financing will yield better results more frequently than you imagine. In the past, prior to the Great

Recession, asking for owner financing caused sellers to believe that you were a vagabonds because banks would not lend to you. The situation has changed however, that it is estimated that 20% of sellers are willing to consider the possibility. If you're able to get owner financing, you must sign a promissory note that specifies how long it will take you to repay the seller and the interest rate you'll receive in the process.

Find a creditor

If you are planning to purchase not just one investment property, but a number of and you'll be taking the time to make an effort to locate an institution that you can establish an ongoing mutually beneficial relationship. This kind of partnership will, ultimately help the two of you to devise the right strategy to ensure that everyone wins not just during the initial meeting, but each subsequent one after that. You should be cautious of real estate agents, but they're not likely to give you the chance to buy the properties that aren't quite what you want in your desires. Keep in mind that the lender will directly be accountable for the distribution of your loan, which is why it is essential to speak with the lender prior to signing a full commitment to anything.Questions you need to ask items like:

What is the number of investors with whom you currently work with?

How many loans could I be able have in one go? ?

What are the best types of real estate investment do you prefer?

These questions , and others like questions will make it simpler for you to select the right lender based on the facts and not sales messages. Keep in mind that if one of you like something about someone, that's perfectly fine, so long as you take the appropriate action and move on from wasting your time both in the short and longer term. If you are unable to locate the loan that's suitable for you, it's essential not to give up and instead work on it. If you want to spend as little upfront as you can, then credit cards, title loans or equity loans based upon other properties that you have are all options but they must be used with care.

Loans for hard money

If you're not interested or eligible for a credit line from a bank, the most suitable option to begin looking for financing is with a loan that is based on hard money. It is an alternative to a traditional loan. It is financed by one or more private investors , instead of an institution that is more conventional in its financial structure. These loans typically last to be used for shorter periods of time than conventional bank loans, and the major portion of the payments that you pay for will involve making principally interest payments until you can make a huge balloon payment comes due at the end, which is primarily with the principal portion of the loan.

Lower barrier for entry The hard money loan is usually very appealing for novice real estate investors due to the fact that getting recognized is more about locating the appropriate property that you can profitable from all angles rather than having a track record of success in real property. If you are looking for the best hard money lender the best place to begin is by contacting the local real estate investment club. If you want to get the truth about the market for real estate in your region there's no better option than a local group that can guide you through the process. Finding a local organization is as simple as logging onto the internet and conducting an online search. It is essential to find an organization to learn from even if aren't in need of help with financing, as there is numerous aspects they can show you.

The lender's considerations Considerations for lenders: When selecting the perfect hard money lender for your needs, it is essential to keep in mind that some specialize in various types of real estate transactions as it's not an ideal idea to invest in an area that you're not knowledgeable about. In addition, you'll be able to locate hard money lenders who willing to lend from an initial lien position this means they'll become the very first person to claim their money back in the event that circumstances go wrong. You might be able to locate hard money lenders willing to accept the second lien position however, it is a harder sell.

In order to understand the types of interest rates you could get from a hard money loan, it is crucial to remember that the amount you pay will differ depending on the region that you reside in as well as the amount of other lenders the lender you're working with. However, the rate will always be greater than the standard rate for a conventional bank loan. It is usually within the 10 to 15 percent range with particulars of the loan going a long ways in bringing the rate up to up to the last few percent. Additionally, the points typically vary between 2 and 4 percent of that the borrower is able to access.

The ratio of value to loan The amount an individual lender with a high risk of lending is willing to loan you will be determined on the loan-to-value ratio. This ratio can be calculated by taking the amount of the loan that is available and then dividing it by the worth of the home when it is fully revamped. The typical amount an ad-hoc lender would accept is something between 65 to 75 per cent of worth of the property when all is done. However, some lenders will decide to set that figure according to what the property's value is in its current condition.

Alternately, you might be able to locate an unsecured lender that is willing to take a larger percentage of the cost and chip into the cost of the project itself. From the perspective of lenders, these kinds of loans are always a risky option and they can expect an investment return up to 20 percent. In these situations, it's possible for a brand new real estate investor in the most suitable deal to get a loan with just a few dollars down, however, that implies that they are worthwhile to consider regardless of the cost.

Requirements for hard money loans in addition to an excellent deal with a low risk as it is When you make an application to a lender who is hard money, you'll be required to have all your ducks lined up. This means that you need to have a credit score of minimum 600 as well as an income/debt ratio which is less than 45 percent, and a credit history free of bankruptcy or foreclosures over at minimum 10 years. Also, you will need to be able prove that you are able to pay for your costs and will have equity in the property which can be used as collateral to prove that you're committed to paying to repay the loan. This can be accomplished by presenting things such as taxes and bank statements and repair estimates, as well as a settlement sheet appraisals of property, along with the agreement of sale. Additionally, you'll want to provide a clear business plan that shows your lender you've got an concept of how to go about acquiring the property at issue. Most lenders will provide answers in less than three weeks.

Crowdfunding a real estate loan

If you're unable to locate an individual hard money lender in your area who you think you'll be able to deal with, you may have better luck pursuing your next investment opportunity online. When you crowdfund an investment property loan, you can anticipate receiving your cash in just 72 hours, and raise as much as 85 percent of your amount you are paying and more. There are a variety of real estate crowdfunding websites available on the internet. Each has its own specifications, but in general you'll require a credit score of minimum 580 and an income-to-debt ratio of less than 50 percent . You also need an outstanding credit history free of bankruptcies, short sales and foreclosures. For the best outcomes in these situations, you're likely to require an experience of at minimum one real estate investment that has been successful in your portfolio.

Real estate websites that use crowdfunding allow anyone interested in becoming a real estate investor to provide the details of the property they are interested in and their plans for the property, their qualifications and any pertinent personal information prior to allowing investment for anyone interested in joining. Individual investors are able to offer any amount of the entire amount and receive a return in proportion to the amount they've invested. The rates for these loans are likely to vary widely between different sites and even though

18 percent is considered to be the most current rate.

Chapter 8: Information Gathering

To establish a professional connection and build a professional relationship with your seller you can start by asking him for his name and after that introduce yourself.

Rationale:

The ability to spell out your name when you introduce yourself could add credibility to yourself . Also, responding to your phone with pleasant, gentle tone creates a welcoming and personal greeting that is excellent. It is also possible to be in control of the conversation because sometimes salespeople find it difficult to discuss certain things. Let's look at the following example:

If the vendor claims they saw your advertisement Make sure to inquire the location where he saw it, or how he came across the business or you, so that you can keep track of your advertisements. If the seller asks questions about the process of real state You can give him some ideas about what you initially did, but don't give everything as the only thing you want to do is to convince them to engage in conversation with you. You could also tell him your most crucial elements in determining the price, if the buyer asks you questions about the price. But , you should not give him more details since the goal is to begin directing the buyer's questions to determine if he is a good fit with your requirements to purchase.

It is important to pause and ponder the seller's words before you decide to respond, as this will allow you to contemplate and think about the message he's delivering and is it is a great way to demonstrate that you're listening to what he's saying. In addition when you ponder and pay attention to his comments or queries, it will suggest that you have a valid reason to believe the opinions from the buyer. It is crucial that, even the seller is not acceptable, don't shout it out , instead try to take the time to listen. Respecting the seller is an excellent beginning to establish trust and a relationship, and is important when buying the property from the seller.

Question You can ask the following query while the seller is discussing the property. "John Do you have a number? I'm on my cell in the event that we are lost or anything." "Thanks, (pause) is this your phone, your home number or office number?"

Rationale:

The seller's working phone numbers is also a good idea to keep in mind once you have built relationships and have signed a contract. This will allow you to receive prompt responses, during business hours, for ease of closing your transaction with the business as well as partners, lenders, and appraisers.

The buyer's motivation and motivation, it's up to you to decide how you will approach the next question. The time to use the "call back" is a good idea particularly if the seller isn't keen to sign the agreement now.

Questions: "John, let me investigate the property as well as the surrounding area. I'll contact you shortly."

Rationale:

It will allow you to build trust and credibility with the seller since it allows you to phone back. The seller will also believe that you're not scared to go out on the premises and purchasing it. Therefore, just be cool and before calling him back, with the intention to steer the conversation.

Scenario: Darrel Street Property

If a seller offers you a phone call in response to a postal mailer that states that he wants to sell his house, try to make an appointment as soon as possible. If he insists to call you after the son moves out of the house, you should wait some time before calling back. If the homeowner appears to be less motivated to sell his property and you want to keep a record of his phone number and follow-up call at a later date.

If the person calls you one year later are able to say that you'll contact instead while you go through the file, while simultaneously, you can build relationships. After a short time, you can you can call him back, then start talking to him about the repairs, and then try to suggest an estimate. There is a chance that he will not compromise or even provide an amount, so ask him to agree to a bargain when you visit and take an examination of the property. When you have received an answer that is positive, proceed.

Take a quick tour of the neighborhood prior to going into the specific property and immediately ask the best price for an instant cash-for-cash deal. If you assume that the value of the property after repairs is 120K to 130K, but with the repairs cost 8K could be the case, you can create a deal of $50,000, if he doesn't give a price before. If he doesn't seem to agree with the price you propose and you are unable to convince him, specify the price. For sure, he'll offer an offer between 55 and 60 thousand.

You might think that a deal that is less than 90K is a good deal but when you get the price, don't be overly enthusiastic. Instead, relax and inform him that you could be able to negotiate a price of 58-59 thousand. When he has agreed to it, go over the agreement document and then let him sign it in a professional manner.

These events show tips on how to speak with sellers, particularly those who will not provide a price or to keep your cool professionally signing the contract being confident that you'll get an affordable deal. This will help you understand that you shouldn't be stressed about closing the deal and the importance of following-up on previous leads. This way, you won't have to guess the buyer's desires for his property.

It is important to be aware of this particular scenario. There are occasions when, just a few days after signature of the agreement the seller may call you and inform you the property could not be sold of the property based on the price you paid. It is possible that you don't know how to respond when you're not familiar with this. However, you need to notify the seller that you've already passed the agreement to your lawyers.

But, you do can choose to call him now to inform him that you're understanding and will call him when you have spoken with your legal team or your lawyer. When you speak to him, be sure to inform him that there are no guarantees for him, such as: "Listen, I understand. However, I'll call you back , but I'm still going to speak with the people. There are no guarantees and they could quite possibly bind you to the current contract But let me know how I might be able to help, and perhaps I can push them to some."

It is important to ask the seller for his price you think the conversation will result in a positive outcome. If he does ask for a for a 9K increment, do not just give up immediately because you might be asked for more. It is recommended that you first consult with your lawyers , and then contact him later the same day or next. What do you think? Who would want to be around anyone who has no an honorable word and without a valid reason? Sure, nobody! However, this is a fact.

From here you can discuss the issue with your team members, and if they accept the price of the new seller and then contact him and tell him: "Listen, my partners are willing to do the deal and are willing to share the difference between the initial fifty-eight thousand you have agreed to in addition to the six hundred seventy-seven thousand you had previously quoted." When the seller is willing to split the cost you can make the deal at 62K or 63K and be sure to confirm that you have made the right offer to him.

It is a good idea to tell him that the last thing you'd like to do is engage your lawyers since you don't want to pay more on the lawyers. Make sure you say it in a pleasant, calm and non-threatening manner.

The question is: "What is the address of John's property? John?"

Rationale:

If you are asking this specific question to the seller you could at the same time access the data, and compare it (comp is defined as houses that were sold in the same region and with the same amount of square footage that have sold in the last twelve months) and then figure out the date of purchase to determine if there's any equity. By doing this, you will be able to determine if the property is worth keeping track of and what direction to take in the discussion.

Questions: "John, can you give me a brief description about this place?"

Rationale:

This question really reveals the real-world appearance of benefit of selling the property as it will be the'meat and potatoes of the good about that specific property. You can tell if the person selling is motivated, or even not only his responses to the questions you'll be asking. It also reminds you that once you have asked you should be attentive and this strengthens your relationship with your seller. Additionally, this will let you communicate more angles and questions when the process of buying a house.

How do you respond when the seller claims that your property's value is 150K , as it was appraised in the last month? Be sure not to be confused as you are aware that most of the time, the selling price isn't important and, in addition the fact that you could simply say that appraisals only work when working with banks. This will tell your seller appraisals are not worthy of the discussion, but at the same time you have made a smart announcement with the perfect timing and at the right time. This is a lesson in how to keep trusting channels of communication with your customers is the most effective way to go about it.

Chapter 9: What to Financing Your Investment

If you've ever had the chance to take an examination of the house costs in your neighborhood you're aware that it will need a substantial amount of money to begin investing in real property. The majority of homes will exceed $100,000, sometimes at a lower cost. Then, you'll need to make repairs to the majority of them before being capable of selling them or lease them out. In the end, you don't necessarily require all the cash in the bank to begin. You can apply for an advance loan from the bank, however this may take some time to process and you'll be accountable for bank fees as well as interest for a period of time until you are capable of selling the property.

As a majority of people do not have enough funds or savings to pay for the purchase of an investment property There are various funding options an investor has the option of choosing from to start. They can help you get the funds you require to purchase the property , as in addition to providing the funds needed to make improvements to the property. However, you need to ensure that you are prepared prior to asking for money.

Portfolio lenders, banks, and a few other lenders are more than willing to offer you a few dollars however, they must ensure that they will be able get their money back. You must be in good financial standing with a business plan and a high credit score, and perhaps an effective marketing strategy before you speak to these organizations.

Good news: that the first property will be the most difficult one to fund. It is necessary to show that you are an excellent candidate to invest in this property without evidence. Once you've completed this a couple of times, bank and the lender will have prove that you are aware of what you're doing and you'll have some money to utilize which makes it more easy to continue.

However, if you're new to the field and don't have a lot of money to start with, it's important to locate a reputable lender who will give you a shot and provide you with the funds you require at a reasonable rate. The various choices you have to choose from include:

Conventional mortgage

The first choice you might want to opt for is a traditional mortgage. It is an excellent option to choose because it lets you start with a specific percentage of down. The conventional mortgage will need a minimum of twenty percent on the property. However, there are alternatives which let you start with a smaller down payment. Conventional mortgages require longer however, they usually offer the lowest interest rates as well as the most favorable conditions to work with.

If you're looking at an ordinary mortgage you're expected to be conducting a lot of the work. You will need to provide many details regarding yourself to assist them determine if you'll be capable of paying the loan back. It is important to prove your earnings background, assets, an acceptable credit score and that you're capable of paying off all the current debts you have while keeping the mortgage you have taken out. Based on the bank you choose to work with There may be additional details they ask for, but begin by filling the application form and then go to the bank.

To increase the chances of getting the money you require, it's ideal to select one you already have a relationship in with. Or at the very least one that is located in your location. This is because they typically will help startups in their community and may already have the necessary information about you they require.

203K loans

Another option could consider and it can be found in the well-known FHA loans. It allows you to be an investor to buy an unfinished property that requires some attention. It will allow you to obtain money to buy the house however, it also will also provide you with funds to repair the house in addition. All of these are all rolled into one loan instead of taking out multiple loans at simultaneously, meaning there will be only one monthly payment to be concerned about.

Hard money

You may also opt to take a finance option called hard money. This option is where you can obtain financing from private individuals and businesses who know you plan investing in property investment with this money. There are various terms you could use when you receive this kind of financing however both you and the other person are able to agree on the particulars between you. The most common terms and conditions associated with this type of funding are:

The loan you get is based on the worth of the property as well as the amount it's worth.

These are typically non-long-term loan. They will require you to repay them in six months to three years.

The interest rate that you pay on this type of loan will be more than traditional loans.

There will be a significant rate of loan on these loans. The result is that you'll need to pay lots of charges on these loans.

The majority of lenders who give the money will ask you to prove the amount of income you earn.

It is likely that the majority of the lenders aren't going to bother to check your credit score, and this transaction won't appear as a credit card transaction.

The loans can be paid in a short time, which is beneficial if you need to get the deal fast.

The majority of lender is aware that you must perform some work on the property prior to being able to get their return on their investment.

If you are looking to buy a home to flip and would like to ensure that you are able to receive the funds quickly, you'll find that the help of a hard money loan is the best option for you. However, you must complete the work on the home completed quickly and then get the house sold quickly because the conditions of these loans aren't likely to last for all the way.

Private money

You may also opt to make use of private money. This type of funding differs slightly from the lending of hard money. The reason for this is that the hard lenders are professional investors and require that you adhere to the guidelines for the investment. If you are a private money lender it is easier to make changes. They are only entering the market and are looking for you to perform the work of real estate, while they earn a money. In certain instances lenders and private individuals may maintain a relationship of trust and vice versa.

Partnerships

Based upon your score on credit as well as your financial situation, it could be difficult to obtain the funds that you require to invest in real estate by yourself. There is a chance that you do not earn enough money, or have excessive debt, or do not have enough funds to make as a downpayment and the bank will deny your application. If that is true with you, it could be worth it to look into joining an alliance with others who want to invest in real estate to improve your chances of receiving funds.

It is likely that banks will consider your request for financing when you're an alliance. This is due to the fact that they are able to have two partners accountable for the payment back. They are also more likely to collect at the very least a portion of the cash back. The bank can take into account the income of each of the parties, making the ratio of debt to income more manageable. Of course, if you're in a partnership it is necessary to share the profits but it will certainly be beneficial in the event that you must take part in the tasks.

Before you make the decision to go in a partnership, it is important to ensure that you choose the right person to enter into this partnership. You want someone with a solid credit rating, earns a decent income, and someone who is willing to assist you in the job. Selecting someone who's not able to meet certain of these factors could cause problems in obtaining the funds you require. It could leave you with the majority of the work for the property and still share the gains.

It is best to use your money to purchase the items since this is the most straightforward, it also costs the least amount since you don't have to pay for interest or other costs, and you'll get to keep the entire profits. However, buying a house can be costly and a lot of real property investors don't have that amount of money to begin their venture. Utilizing different types of investments can aid in getting the cash you need to you can buy your house either by renting it out or even flip it and begin earning money from real property.

Chapter 10: Flipping Tips

Flipping houses requires more than just finding the perfect property in the proper place. It's a start to your strategy, however, you must allow people to be enticed by the home. What's at stake is ensuring that the home is worth more to earn you a return on your investment. This involves turning your home into something that people are likely to want to buy.

If you don't find something in your home that you are drawn to, how will anyone else be able to see the potential? There are methods to make your home neutral enough to draw the attention of a large audience but still keep it comfortable and welcoming.

There are ten ways experts suggest flippers make an increase in the value of their homes that buyers are willing to pay what you offer:

Create the illusion of space. It would be great to have homes that had enough room for everyone to spread out. But, this costs money. It is possible in order to "create space" to help people appreciate the benefits to live in your house. For instance, could you switch a few rooms to provide an office, and you still have enough bedrooms to accommodate the family of four? Maybe, you can create an outside space that is welcoming and makes a family feel the inside as inviting since they will spend much of their time outdoors. You can also create space by knocking down the walls. The walls that are not structural could be removed to make the kitchen bigger.

Curb appeal ranks high among the top suggestions because it's the primary factor that makes buyers want to reconsider. If you have an open house or put up photos online, buyers are looking to see if the home is appealing from the outside, as well as inside. This can mean pruning, tiny adjustments to the landscaping as well as possible adjustments to the colour of the house are necessary. More curb appeal give a house and the more easy you will find it to persuade potential buyers to stop, walk inside, and take a look at what your home has to provide. Think about replacing the front door. The fresh paints and front doors can improve curb appeal. A well-designed front door will let in more light.

If you can, alter your interior design to allow more light. Do you have the funds to install an outdoor door located in an area that has only one door to the outside? Do you have the option of installing an awning because you need to rebuild your house? Any modifications that allow more light into the house should be considered, however other elements shouldn't be sacrificed to increase the light. For instance, if a bathroom requires new flooring, do it instead of an skylight. If your budget won't permit the renovation of your bathroom, think about the skylight option that is more affordable.

It is important to reduce the amount you spend on renovations as low as you can, without sacrificing value. If you live in a house constructed before the 1980s You should consider new windows in the event that windows that are more energy efficient are already in place. Make the most eco-friendly choices you can when it comes to your house, but without spending a fortune. Making upgrades to appliances that are outdated and squeezing the efficiency of the house will boost the value of your home and make it easier to sell the property. If the appliances aren't modern or efficient in energy use, the buyer will have to buy new appliances. So, save them the hassle and ask for an extra portion of the price of purchase.

Brokers say that spending between $600 and $900 on flooring in an entire home can boost the value by at least $2,000. Modernized flooring, repairing scratches in flooring and fixing damage can help in improving the appeal of a house.

Spending $500 on bathrooms could increase the value. A new bathroom and caulking the tub, sink, as well as the backsplash can enhance the appearance of an older bathroom. Cleaning out rusty stains, and updating knobs on the cabinet, door pulls and faucets are all ways you can enhance the look of your bathroom.

Kitchens are exactly the same. It is possible to replace Formica counters by acquiring new ones however, often, the heavy cleaning of cabinets and doors, as well as re-aligning them, and applying a fresh stain to the look of the kitchen. You'd like to give it a fresh look without investing a lot of money.

Colors for walls that are neutral are important. The painting of every room in the house is essential. Fresh paint gives a fresh "look." The white paint can turn yellow and become filthy with time. Thus, a fresh coat of off white or white paint will really assist. These neutral colors are also cheap. A 5-gallon bucket can be bought for less than $50 at certain stores. The trim needs to be a different shade however, it should be neutral.

Create a tidy closet and close to your front entrance. There are two main reasons that require space in the closet for their possessions, and a space to store their shoes, coats and other outdoor gear. If you can, create the mudroom from an garage, and the space for visitors coats to be hung at the door to the front. If there's no garage, create a welcoming front door however, it must be well-organized. Even Kraftmaid in the closet is better than an empty space.

If you are unsure about something there is a need to get it repaired.

Let's say you've picked an old-fashioned house from the 1950s. The woodwork is beautiful however, the wallpaper is outdated. Take it off the wall. The market isn't for wallpapers, especially in the case of 60 plus years old wallpaper. Re-stain the woodwork, keeping it, the wood, and ensuring there aren't any gaps, and do get rid of things that buyers will not appreciate. If something appears to be a problem to you, or "unfixed" in your eyes, it is likely to be bother the buyer.

The buyer will take a look at the aesthetics of the home versus the foundation as well as the roof and date of the water heater, however the inspector will record the details of all those items. In addition, it could be costly to not make improvements or address unsightly areas. The value you add to your home, which is why it's best to do all or none. It is possible that you will not be able to replace every single toilet sink, tub, or toilet however, you can make use of caulking, deep cleaning and polish to rejuvenate old fixtures. If the bathroom appears like new and is done properly it is possible to get a ROI on your investment.

Chapter 11: Transfer of Title in A Will

In many cases, a deed and title to real estate property is transferred according to the instructions from the will. This is the method you use to purchase your first property or an option to make a title claim on the property you purchased from the previous heirs to the property.

Holographic wills are written by hand in the testator's (the person who is writing their last will and testament) handwriting. Holographic wills can be valid provided that they are written by the testator's handwriting and are signed by the testator. Certain states, like California are not required to have a witness to the holographic will, however other states like Maryland will require witnesses be present.

Nuncupative wills are written wills that are executed before witnesses or witnesses. Some states only accept nuncupative wills, and, even then, they require witnesses from multiple parties and the witnesses must sign the will in writing soon after. In order to amend a will an additional document, called the codicil (from the Latin codex) must be written and then attached with the will. it is possible to discover both the original will as well as a more recent codicil.

In the will, the gift of real estate is known as a devise whereas giving personal property is known as a will or legacy. It is interesting to note that when the US took over the concept of devise from English statute, it used the term devises as representing EITHER personal or real property within the US Uniform Probate Code. For US users the term devise means an offer that is property that is real OR private property.

TITLE INSURED

Title insurance is often required by lenders, and in other cases, it's optional. It is typically priced at $1000 however it can range from the range of a few hundred dollars to several thousand dollars. Contrary to other developed countries in the world, the US government offers hardly any assurances regarding the validity of the title. The local government takes note of each property sale and collects a recording and an administration fee. The title's condition and imperfections is the responsibility of the purchaser to determine.

In 1868 in 1868, the Pennsylvania Supreme Court ruled in favor of Muirhead in the Watson v. Muirhead case. Muirhead worked as a conveyancer of transactions, a professional who was responsible for conducting an abstract of title' or search of title records through public documents. Muirhead discovered an unpaid lien on the title, and handed it over to an attorney to get a legal opinion. The attorney informed him that the judgment wasn't an appropriate lien. After the property was bought from the purchaser, it auctioned off in the Sheriff's sale which is a court-ordered auction of a property that was foreclosed. If the mortgage lien was in the title that is, the bank or lender would be able to foreclose the property and hold its own auction or short sale. In this instance the sale was called a Sheriff's auction to pay off different types of debt. The case was taken before the Supreme Court to find the conveyancer accountable, but it was decided that the Supreme Court found that Muirhead was not responsible because there was no evidence of negligence as he relied upon an attorney's advice. Disappointed by the ruling Landowners petitioned to the Pennsylvania State Legislature to come up with better legislation and in 1874 lawmakers passed legislation that allowed the creation of title insurance. The first company to offer title insurance was founded in Philadelphia by an organization of transaction conveyancers whose sole purpose was to safeguard "the people who purchase mortgages and real estate against the loss resulting from deficient title, liens, and encumbrances".

Title Insurance can be described as an indemnity policy that protects against problems with the title. This is usually requested by a lender and is paid by the homeowner however, the cost could be split to the sellers in a market for buyers. The title company decreases its risk by conducting an investigation of the title looking through the title chain (whom it transferred the title to throughout the duration of the property usually 60 years earlier) to ensure that there are no flaws in the title. Abstracts of properties are a document that contains the chain title and historical liens however, it could be insufficient and may be incorrect. Consequently, the title insurer must do a deeper analysis by examining additional sources, such as tax records, wills and testaments of previous owners, and earlier court judgements.

Common title defects can lead to claims from descendants, court judgements (such as post-divorce settlements of property) as well as liens, inaccuracies on public records, or even forgeries in public records and boundary or survey issues , such as easements or encroachments.

The cost for title insurance is due at the time of closing, but it is possible to pay before closing. What you receive at the end of the day from the title firm is referred to as an title commitment or a title binder. It states that the insurance company will protect the property upon settlement or closing and issue an official title insurance contract which protects lenders and buyers.

There is a chance that you will hear about a lender's policy or the homeowner's policy. they're both the same with regards to title insurance, except that the lender policy will cover the equity of the lender within the home, whereas the homeowner's policy will cover the equity of the new owner in the property based on the time the title defect was discovered and the amount of the principle was paid. Both policies are usually paid by the buyer.

Title insurance, however, only covers items with a an open record. This is something that title insurance companies have studied prior to the time they purchase it in order to reduce their risk. The concept of constructive notice is that the entire world is bound by the information about the title conveyance once the conveyance is recorded publicly and the owner is able to take possession. Therefore, a title insurance company would not like to be held accountable for defects in title that weren't documented publicly.

Title insurance is not able to include a list of exceptions , which includes the situation where purchasers move into their residence and discover that someone is living on their home particularly when there is no official record of tenure, such as lease. Another exemption is a mechanic's lien issued by a contractor who didn't get paid or an equivalent lien that was not recorded by the office of the county clerk.

New homeowners and potential buyers are able to purchase what's known as extended coverage, which includes these exceptions and more. The title insurance provider will spell out the conditions an extended insurance policy will cover and will cost several thousand dollars for additional coverage.

For instance, First American Title Insurance Company (NYSE FAF) Standard (basic) policy will cover the forged, incorrect or unreported title defects which are recorded found in the PUBLIC record, for example:

* Impersonation and forgery;

* Incompetence or capacity of a person;

* Deeds not joined by a required party (co-owner or spouse, heir corporate officer, spouse, corporate officer, spouse or business partners);

* Unknown (but noted) the prior lien or mortgage

* Unknown (but not recorded) easement or usage restriction;

Legally incorrect or inaccurate descriptions;

* Insufficient right to access and

* The deed was not recorded properly.

The extended coverage policy of the company has some other exceptions which are not recorded included in the public record, like:

* Off-record matter like claims for prescriptive easements

*Deeds to land that includes the buildings that encroach on the other land;

* Incorrect survey*;

* Silent (off-record) lien (such as mechanics or tax estate liens); and

* Prior-existing infractions of subdivision ordinances, Zoning laws, or CC&R's**

When you have read the information included in the basic and expanded coverage, you'll feel satisfied that you know how liens are defined, what adverse possession and prescriptive easements!

*Surveys (covered before) could need to be paid prior to when extended coverage is approved. A thing to be aware of that the buyer is accountable for paying the surveyor.

**We will discuss the zoning ordinances as well as CC&Rs in the future to give you a full overview of what to keep an eye for.

Certain of the most expensive items are covered under the premium product line known as The First American EAGLE Policy. What a fantastic marketing idea, don't you think? The first American Eagle? However, this policy also covers other exceptions, including the unfortunate scenario when you purchase a house that has 3 bedrooms only to discover that the third room was not allowed and the local government obliges you to take the room down. If you are a smart buyer when a seller claims they've added a new room on their property, you must inquire if the addition is allowed. If the seller is lying and then is liable. You can also make a complaint and confirm the truth by visiting the city or county website and looking through the property's building permits.

For closing this section of policy details for First American Title Insurance Company their eagle insurance policy (as of the year 2018) contains the following limitations:

* Forgery post-policy;

* Removing improvements because of a lack of a the building permits (subject to deduction);

* Post-policy construction of improvements carried out by an adjacent neighbor on the insured land and

* Dimensions and location of the land insured (survey is not necessary).

The Uniform Commercial Code (UCC) is a set of rules for business established in the 1950s which regulate financial contracts involving the personal possessions of individuals (not real estate in itself). In the title search , and therefore within the report on title one could come across a

UCC-1 statement that is abridged financial statement that outlines the particular personal property of the property, which has a lien since the collateral was utilized to secure financing, for instance. It is essential to know if the seller says they will include furniture from their home in the sale, however the title search indicates that the furniture was used to provide collateral to secure an individual loan.

Your agent or lender may suggest a title insurance firm. Be aware that according to RESPA (Real Estate Settlement Procedures Act) they are not able to require that you choose one title insurer over the other. The title insurers responsible for the largest portion of market are Fidelity National Financial First American Corporation, Old Republic National Title Insurance Company as well as Stewart Title Guaranty Company but there are numerous smaller local title insurance companies to pick from.

It is crucial to remind readers from Iowa readership that Iowa banned the title insurance industry in 1947, and in 1987 created this non-profit Iowa Finance Authority in order to provide title guarantees to a property. The procedure is that the Iowa buyer will pay an amount of between $100 and $150 as a premium to receive the assurance of a title that is clean to the state. Then, they the buyer would pay between $400 and 600 for an Abstract firm to perform the title search as well as an attorney who will certify your title (attorneys charge between $300 and $400 to verify the title). Overall, you're getting around $600-800 for a property worth $500,000 which is the lowest cost in any state. Comparatively to Texas and California buyers can expect to shell out around $2500. However it is true that it is true that the procedure in Iowa takes longer than when working with an insurance company for private title that is not in the state. In addition, approximately 50% of the people who purchase in Iowa opt to work with title insurance companies outside of state.

THE CLOSING PROCESS

There are some states with "wet closing' rules where the transfer and settlement of deeds can only take place once closing fees have been paid by all the participants and they have signed closing documents. This is different from "dry closing" or "closing within escrow' states in which settlement and signing of documents could be completed and the title company is given the option of holding onto the deed until final costs of the closing have been paid.

When closing a transaction, these participants meet in a particular address or in the office of the title company:

The seller, buyer, and their representatives.

The lawyer for the Lender.

Lawyers for buyers and sellers (optional).

A Settlement Officer (title representative) In certain states, there is a law that requires the supervision of an attorney at closing. In other states, the title representative can also be an attorney.

The title representative informs both the buyer and seller of the closing charges that need to be transferred through the certified money (money order or certified check wire) prior to closing or upon closing. The title representative allocates the funds in accordance with those closing papers (for instance allocating a percentage for the commission paid to the agent). The closing documents are then signed, the deed transferred and keys are exchanged.

Escrow accounts are third-party account which is not connected to any of the tenets of contract negotiations that keeps the funds in reserve up until the time the contract has been signed executed. In the real estate industry an escrow account usually managed by an escrow representative who could be an attorney, an entity that deals in title or a seller broker. The escrow broker by law is not allowed to mix or mixing funds from escrow accounts with their personal bank accounts. They are also legally barred from conversion or using the escrow money to pay for their expenses (with the intention of paying the account back in the future). The escrow representative is known as the settlement officer, which is the neutral third party. They are still required to be paid and their fees are paid at the time of closing.

We've talked about the closing documents in the past and also to remind you, the closing documents that need to be signed prior to settlement being able to be completed are:

Sale agreement between buyer seller.

Listing agreement between the seller as well as their representative.

A contract for brokerage between the buyer as well as their representative.

A mortgage loan agreement is a contract between the buyer and the lender.

The title contract is between the buyers and title representatives.

A cooperative arrangement for brokerage between sellers and buyers agents.

Furthermore, there are various disclosure forms that must be handed out to the loan provider prior the completion of the settlement. These forms are mandated by law since the most painful aspect of closing on a house is financing. They are required by law. Lender legally required forms for disclosure include:

Estimate of the Loan: Estimation of all expenses related to the loan provided within 3 business days after submitting for the loan.

Closing Disclosure form Final closing costs, which includes the due amounts and the credits that were paid, such as credits for earnest money that was paid. The form must be provided within three business days prior to closing.

The new form that's 5 pages long. It replaces the previously used form referred to by the name of Settlement Statement, also known as HUD-1 form.

Escrow Closing Notice: Issued within three business days prior to the closing of an escrow account, if it was established by the lender.

The Mortgage Service Transfer If the existing mortgage is transferred to the NEW lender it is a requirement to have an additional document to document the transfer.

A partial payment notice: Presented to a borrower upon the loan on an already owned property has been transferred, sold, assigned or transferred in any other way. It happens when a buyer takes over the mortgage on an existing seller (which was partly paid).

The Seller Net Sheet will be a document that is given to the seller's agent by providing estimates of net proceeds for the seller after expenses such as brokerage commissions and accrued interest, taxes, and insurance have been paid. While a seller may be selling their home for $350,000 however, the net proceeds may be much higher than $300,000. this information is useful to ensure that there are no unexpected costs for the seller prior to closing.

If things do not get settled prior to or at the time of closing and if one party is in default on the agreement the escrow agency will disburse the earnest funds according to the release of deposit agreement.

Chapter 12: What is A Reverse Mortgage?

If you're 62 or over, and have property with a substantial sum in equity (the difference between the value of your house as well as the amount you are obligated to pay) You may be eligible for reverse mortgage.

Example: If your home is valued at $100,000 and you have an outstanding loan of $30,000 to the home, you'd have equity of $70,000.

100,000 (value of the house)

$35,000 (debt to the house)

$700,000 (cash or "equity" in the home)

This type of loan is known as reverse mortgage as instead of paying monthly installments to a lender to pay off the debt you have to pay the lender performs"reverse. "reverse" and offers you money.In this way, each month, the equity in your home is diminished.

Reverse mortgages and the conventional "forward" mortgage can result in debt.In the conventional mortgage, you've borrowed a specific sum of cash from a lender to buy your home.

The amount will be paid in installments over time, and eventually, you will have your house free and clear of debts if you own the house for long enough time to achieve that.With the conventional mortgage loan the amount of debt is reduced and the equity rises.

When you take out a reverse loan, you're borrowing against the equity in your home, which will increase the amount you owe the home.Therefore you bring the equity amount down and the amount of amount of debt up.In this instance, the debt is increased , and the equity is reduced.

You can choose to make monthly withdrawals through the reverse mortgage program, or withdraw in lump amounts, or even a combination of both.

Since you've decided not to market your house and "cash out" the cash you're using is borrowed by the lender and not yours. Interest (what the lender is charging for the privilege to utilize the money) is due only at the expiration of the loan term, when it will be completely paid.

The reverse mortgage lends money against a specific proportion of your equity and once the amount owed exceeds the maximum amount permitted in addition to the expenses to ensure the reverse mortgage's security and the loan payments end.You as the owner can remain in the property to the length want, or so long as you're physically capable.

If you decide to leave the property, action has to occur within a specified amount of time in order to meet the reverse mortgage (check the guidelines of the lender for the precise amount of time permitted). The reverse mortgage will normally be repaid by selling or refinancing the house.

In short it is possible for a reverse mortgage to allow you to remain within your home and use the equity.For homeowners who have significant equity but are lacking cash or savings and are looking to reduce the equity in their home might be a feasible solution.Homeowners can receive regular income from their lender through payments.

The benefits of a reverse mortgage

You can live at home.

There is no payment until the time you are done.

You've got extra money to pay for monthly expenses such as medical bills, and other expenses that could be required.

A reverse mortgage could be the ideal solution for cash-flow issues however, it's an extremely complex product that can be difficult to understand for people and the fees are quite high when compared against other options for loans that you could be offered.

A lot of companies target aggressively seniors, but fail to provide all details.Make sure that you're working with a lender who spends the time to make sure you understand the details and discuss the details with your family and friends Make sure you make sure that all expenses are in written form!

Does my home qualify?

To be eligible for a reverse mortgage , your residence must be in one or more of the following categories:

Single-family homes

A property with 2 to 4 units

Manufactured home (built in 1976 or later)

Condominium or townhome

(Co-ops do not qualify)

What happens if I am already a homeowner?

To allow reverse mortgages to be in place the mortgage that is that is currently in place on the property has to have been cleared off.Reverse mortgage guidelines

155

stipulate that the mortgage must be placed in the primary mortgage position (no other loans prior to it).

The mortgage that was originally secured can be paid off in a variety of different methods, which include but are not restricted to:

Utilizing a portion of the proceeds from this reverse loan.

With the money taken from accounts of savings, or any other liquid asset.

Assistance from an individual from the family.

What kinds of reverse mortgages do you have available?

The most commonly employed in the present is called the Home Equity Conversion mortgage sometimes referred to as the HECM.This kind of reverse mortgage was developed and is managed through HUD. U.S. Department of Housing and Urban Development (HUD).

It is important to note that the HECM is not supported by the federal government, but is a loan provided by a private institution and is insured through the Federal Housing Administration (FHA).The borrower is required to pay an annual insurance cost of 1.25 percent of the current loan balanceto pay an insurance premium.This loan's premium is paid out of the equity balance, and is not required been paid by cash.

The insurance covers the lender in two ways.First in the event that the lender isn't able to meet the monthly payments according to the terms the borrower has been promised then the insurance provided by the government acts as a security net.Second in the event that the worth of the house (at when it was sold sale) is not sufficient to cover the loan's balance the insurance fund of the government covers the remaining balance , and homeowners or their descendants are liable nothing.

The Private Reverse Mortgage can be described as the second kind of mortgage available however it is smaller and less common.These reverse mortgages can be backed by private lenders that provide these loans.

They're like HECMs but they aren't covered by the same rules. These types of reverse mortgages can be utilized to finance homes with a greater value, however both kinds of reverse mortgages are subject to certain limitations.Consult with many lenders to learn about the different kinds of loans that are available and the best way to apply them to your specific situation.

Chapter 13: Sellers Of Expired

Listings Are A Unique Breed

As I've mentioned previously success in the field of real estate is a lot to be done with identifying an area of interest and paying as much focus on the area as you can. If you attempt to focus on all kinds of subjects, you loose your focus and you'll never be able to accomplish one thing successfully. For me, it was dealing with expired products. Yes, I received numerous referrals from my friends. Sure, I was able to pick up some customers at the open house, or the occasional floor call. But, the particular area I was most interested in included working with owners who had their listings expired.

Let me start by telling you a bit about the specialness that is"expired" clients "expired" clients. They're a unique kind of client. Think about the sources. The seller has had his house listed through a different agent. This agent did not succeed in selling the property. The agent LET the house go to auction... that is considered a crime by its own in my humble opinion.

One of the great things about working with sellers who have the expired listings is that they're usually highly driven. If you make an appointment, you'll be able to certain that you are dealing with someone who truly wants to sell. When you distribute massive mailings, it's like casting a large net in the hopes of catching a decent fish. Why not concentrate on specific areas? If you are able to target the listings that have expired You can be sure that the odds are high that you'll be dealing with a motivated seller.

It is equally important to recognize that it is likely that this seller is angry at the very least, and exhausted at the very best. They probably signed up for the listing with high expectations. They might have been promised numerous things, but they were never provided. They've spent hours cleaning their homes and in good condition for showings, but it haven't produced anything. The only thing they lost was market time.

They could still be hopeful. If that's the case, you'll be fortunate to get the chance to visit them and help them remain optimistic.

However If they're like the majority of sellers with expired listings, they'll have lost trust in realtors. They will hold every negative experience they had with their previous agent and pass it on to you.

I was fortunate enough to have worked with a variety of sellers who were listed, not only once however, twice or more, by other realtors. They were the most difficult sellers, as you could imagine. Let me mention that their view of realtors was very modest... Maybe less than used car salesmen , and lawyers for slick injuries.

It is your responsibility to alter those. You will have the chance to prove that you stand out from the crowd. It is that you really want to support them. If you don't really care that much, then this may not be the right line of work for you.

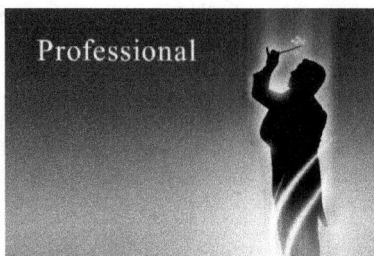
Professional

I'm not saying you need to be cozy and warm. I'm simply telling you to be able to identify with the unique circumstances of an owner whose home did not sell.

You are the expert. It's fine to be open and honest about your thoughts regarding the pricing of your products and other marketing tactics. It all comes down to shipping... however I'm going to digress. Let's look at the actual system so that you'll know what it takes to reach the table with these vendors at all!

Be the professional

My mother was always a proponent of that the Golden Rule. Treat people the way you would want to be treated. I have always kept this in mind both in my personal and professional life. I've always made an effort to treat colleagues and clients like I would like to be treated. When I sold my first home around 1995, I phoned mom of a close friend of mine, who was working working in the field of real estate. She was secretary for many years at her office for real estate prior to taking the plunge to get her license. She was just starting out when she put my house on the market. I can remember the enthusiasm she displayed when she visited and signed the sale contract. But, after an entire week, the situation changed.

I felt as if that I had been a collection of dollar signs for her. The way she sounded was disconcerting whenever I called. She was not able to fully answer my concerns and instead of ignored me most times. The house was sold quickly, and she kindly handed me keys to me and took her check. I've never felt very comfortable about distributing her the commission, which she split with the agent of the buyer.

	S/F HOUSE	COMMERCIAL LAND
OWNERS' VALUE:	$78,000	$130,000
DEBT:	$26,000	$ 60,000
EQUITY:	$52,000	$ 70,000
BOOT:	$18,000	- 0 -
BALANCE:	$70,000	$ 70,000

I kept that memory in my the back of my mind when I started working as a real estate agent. I didn't want my clients to feel that they were a burden. However I'm going off topic here.

My reason for discussing"the" Golden Rule is this: In the case of prospecting for business I was looking to prospect in the same way as I would like to be approached.

I did not want to be the kind of realtor that neighbors and friends avoided because they were afraid that they might be asked to refer them.

I did not want to be the real estate agent who calls to make calls, and then calls.

I did not want to be the professional real estate agent who has everything the right thing to say and has an answer for every question.

I just needed to find another method. The method I've found is one that I'd like to show readers in this book. First of all, I was a guardian of this method with my entire life. I learned a few fundamentals from an experienced realtor, but I then modified and customized it to reflect who am and the way I conduct business.

The system is effective. It's not only effective however, it also allows you to search for and get expired listings without becoming an inconvenience. It displays professionalism and trustworthiness. It demonstrates that you are a true gentleman or woman.

Do you want to increase your real estate company exponentially? Do you desire the ability to work as an actual professional working in a normal working schedule? Are you looking to regain control over your life at home and have the freedom you desire of being able to have a constant stream of income?

Yes, you are able to get there, and you will, when you implement this easy and effective method. In this book I'll give you the essential tools for building an empire of listing. Make yourself the best agent within your office. I guarantee you that when you implement this system notice how quickly people will be talking within your office. Others realtors will be asking what you're doing. They'll talk to you. Prepare yourself. However, who cares. You'll be smiling the entire journey to your front desk in order to collect your commission check!

It is truly a tried and tested method. From having only two listings, to having fourteen listings within the first one month after I started using the system. The number continued to increase. Agents would ask me what I did differently. I would inform them that I was targeting expired listings but I wouldn't say how.

I was so sceptical that I'd visit the office after dark, even though no one was in the office and make duplicates of documents that I am sharing with you. I was afraid that someone would steal the information I was putting out and take the my business I was after.

Yes, I am aware. The reality is that there is enough work for every person. It doesn't matter how many realtors are there in the world, if you're skilled in what you do and you perform it with integrity You will be successful regardless of what.

Are you ready to go all out? Are you becoming impatient? I'm sure not! We'll see!

Chapter 14: Real Estate Divestiture

If the purpose for the contest is acquisition of property so why not should you think about divesting? "Why should I dispose of what I've spent so much time and effort to acquire?" A great question that has many solutions.

Every month in January, Pascagoula, Mississippi, "Smokey" Joe West sits down in his office to complete each year's "culling." I first became aware of this procedure when I contacted Smokey in January of last year. With a soft southern accent, he told me the process was to evaluate each family within his collection. With between 50 and 60 homes, it could be a daunting task. I was curious about the way he ranked them. "Let's look at one home as an example" he explained. "I compute the numbers in relation to the amount I initially put into it and the amount the house has cost me during the period of holding and the amount of cash flow it's thrown off until now. If the numbers look good and it's a winner, it's worth keeping. If the numbers look somewhat shaky, I'll put it on the'review' pile. If the numbers are not good then the file goes in the 'to go pile. After I'm finished with the math I review the review pile a second time to review it in relation to the level of management it's required. If it's not a waste of my time, I'll retain it. If the property, or the tenants have caused a troublesome experience, it will be disposed of." On the outside, Smokey is a soft-spoken friendly and gentle. You may consider him to be a little slow. But you're wrong! The brain of his patient is moving at a brisk pace and never ceases. He's a wonderful friend and has assisted me in more ways than he can count.

Try a few times to purge your portfolio, and you'll soon understand the need to divest. The most important aspect of selling could be the tax consequences. Check your tax calculations with your CPA before putting up the sign for sale. Once you have a better understanding of the tax implications of a cash-only sale it is possible to conduct a few test trials with owner financing, exchanging 1031 and trades with buy-back provisions or any of the many ways to minimize the tax burden. Does the property you own to invest or meet the requirements of dealers in Tax Code? Consider a lot of thought on the reason you're motivated or have to sell your property. Prior to defining your requirements, it can help you increase the number of potential buyers who are interested in your home. More flexible and open your approach to thinking and the faster you'll be free of title.

A cash-only sale may seem perfect, but after a review together with the CPA it seems that the government could take more than you are willing to sell. We'll look at alternatives to get rid of the title. Give a donation to a charitable organization that is a recognized charity and you will receive an annuity for the rest of your life. (Not anything I've done, however I know the principles). Think about establishing a trust for you and your grand and children kids and funding the trust using the property. Think about selling a half interest to your current tenant. Join some friends who also have an interest in properties in the vicinity. Let everyone contribute a house to a trust and hand the management of the properties over to a reputable management company , with the expectation that you'll sell the property in the next eight years and then divide the profits. If you think about it as well as "idea tracking" you can think of a myriad of ways to manage the control and management of your home.

1031 EXCHANGES "No profit or loss can be recognized on exchanging property for use in a trade or business , or as an investment purposes, only to purchase property similar to it to be used to be used in productive ways in a business or investment." (Code Section. 1031) (Code Sec. 1031) advised to go through the entire code section 1031 and the case law that relates to the rules and usages of the section. There are a variety of seminars and books that cover the topic. You should attend one or two seminars in case you're not sure the process. An in-depth discussion of this is not the subject of this guide.

A tool that I utilize frequently is beneficial in balancing the equity on any exchange. It is known as"the "T" Bar. It's easy to build and is easy to remember. Start with a blank sheet of paper, and trace lines across the page , about 2 inches above the bottom. Then, divide the page in half using an upward line drawn from between the top and the bottom. Then you'll have your "T" bar. On the left side , write the following words:

THE VALUE OF THE OWNER

EXISTING DEBT

EQUITY:

BOOT:

BALANCE:

This is the form. Let's look at a real-world scenario to see how the form can be used. There is a house that you live in that has a loan balance of $30,000 and owner's value of $78,000. You propose to trade your house in exchange for commercial property worth $130,000, with an outstanding credit of $60,000 (and an agreement to lease the land in place for $900/month - enough to pay your PITI while the tenant is bound to purchase the land in three years for $150,000). Let's even out the transaction using the next "T" The bar.

The secret to balancing exchanges is knowing and using your "T" bars. The first step is to draw and label it. Then fill in the provided information (the existing debt and The Owner's Value) for both properties. After that, subtract the owner's Value to calculate the equity line for both properties.

Whatever equity is larger or more substantial, write "-0--" to the Boot line, and bring the equity amount up to the line at the bottom ("Balance"). Whatever the balance number (in this instance $70,000) place that number into "Balance" within the second column (in this instance under the house column in the S/F).

The final step. At this point , the only open box is that in the column for single families next to"BOOT. "BOOT." Subtract the equity sum ($52,000 in our instance) from the balance value ($70,000) then the final answer for the boot box in the S/F home column is $18,000.

That means you have to put in $18,000 worth of something to be able to negotiate. It could be paper, cash or any of the other things. It is now possible to make a balance on any transaction size using the use of any number of legs. This "T" Bar has proved to be an excellent and profitable instrument for me.

179

Paper as a diving tool Real estate-secured paper is the focus of the second part of this guide. You will be able to learn the basics of Paper or even add it to the one that you already have. The majority of the papers I've ever purchased was made for selling real estate and not to make the Paper. There are numerous ways to arrange Paper for your benefit in the event that you decide to sell your property and keep the loan in the hands of the prospective buyer. Here are a few suggestions.

Conclusion

This article was a pleasure to create and share with greater than 12 million consumers and buyers of property. It took me a while and having to go over the procedure more than handful of times to become an well-informed consumer, but in the end I felt more nervous than was required by the circumstance. I learned from my experience and decided to apply for an estate license to save another 3percent when I purchase and sell myself properties. It's not necessary to obtain an actual license to sell real estate however, but Rich Dad never got a real estate license. I hope this series has captured the excitement that I experienced and am sure you had when reading The Rich Dad Poor Dad classic book and provided some more information about the procedure of purchasing or selling a property to build your portfolio!

Below is a checklist to guide you through the procedure. This book is full of information, however that's because there's a ton of information that most traditional books for motivational reading do not contain. If you've taken the time to develop an understanding of the basics and understand the sections you should refer to to refresh yourself and you've achieved many things in a brief amount of time.